MAX AND CHARL

CW01665573

as told by Max

Pauline Murray

Dedicated to the memory of Charles Bower and Max

All proceeds from the sale of this book go to
the ALS Society of New Brunswick and Nova Soctia (alsnbns.ca).

Copyright ©2023 Pauline Murray
All rights reserved.

Cat illustrations:
Thanks and credits to the contributing artist,
a young man who befriended Charlie and loved Max

Design by David W. Edelstein
Additional illustrations by Freepik.com and Vecteezy.com

Published by Living the Gift Publications
ISBN: 978-0-9952973-3-3

Hello, my name is Max.

I am a black and white cat who lives with this human called Charlie.

I came to be with him several years ago.

This is my story.

I live on a farm with other cats, a dog named Tag, and other small critters.
I think the big red barn is where I was born.

Sometimes, I don't get my share of the food that is put outside for all of the animals that live here.

One day, during my daily rounds and explorations of the neighbourhood, I decide to venture up over the hill, which seems like it will take me forever.

Wow, what a surprise to see this big house, with humans hanging out on the front porch, and they also have a red barn.
I wonder if they have lots of cats here, too.

I decide to have a look around to see if they feed any animals they might have.

To my surprise, they have lots of bird feeders around the property. When desperate, seed is good. It's a nice filler, and I can also eat a bird or two.

My humans from the red barn down over the hill scold me for bringing dead birds to the doorstep.
I don't get why they are so mad over a dead bird. I thought they would be happy for me.

This is a paradise! What more could a country cat want?
After digesting a lot of bird seed and no live birds, I hang around for the day. I also find a great fresh water supply — a huge pond just in back of the red barn.

The possibilities for this cat are endless!
There don't appear to be any other animals to bug me or take over my food supply — wow!

But all of a sudden, from the corner of my eye, I spot another cat – a big, all-white female, and does she look like a mean one.

Oh no.

I will just show her who is moving in to this paradise — ME.

I will show her who is going to be the new boss around here, but first I will scurry up this big maple tree in the front yard to spy on her.

Of course, this is what smart cats do.

I find out that the humans who live here call her Alice, and she is from my old barn down the hill.

Oh no, she could be my sister – not good.

Okay, I need to take stock. I want food.
Better than fighting off all of the other cats, dogs and other critters down the hill.

Who feeds her?

I need to keep an eye out while still exploring MY new domain.

This Alice cat seems to hang around the smaller house by the pond and down the lane.

I will check this out for food.

Day three, and I haven't been home to the old barn.

I think I like this better — at least I have lots of fresh water, bird food, and the occasional bird and squirrel to eat.

And I think I have met the resident human — his name is Charlie.

He has patted me a few times and told me to go home.

I guess he doesn't know that I have decided to take up residence on the hill, and maybe in his house. I feel a nice connection with his hand.

So I will ignore his words.

I think he really likes me, and that we are going to be good friends.

But he doesn't know it yet.

Wow there are so many people at this place!
In the big house that goes on forever, there are always lots of nice people sitting outside in this screened off area.
It kind of stinks in there, but I'm not sure what it is.

They all like me, and I sit beside one to await a little pat on the head, or even better, a tummy rub.

I could just hang out in this new place, but I need to get some of the special food that Alice gets.
Maybe I am getting a little fussy — I don't eat so much of the bird food under the big old tree.

I am exploring all kinds of new areas these days.

I still haven't gone back down the hill to my first home – did I tell you there is a big pond here that has fresh water?

And I think there are fish in there, too! I wonder what they taste like.

I really have to stay out of sight of Alice and the human called Charlie.

The red barn that looks like the one I was born in is where Charlie spends a lot of his time. I must try and sneak in to find out what is in there.

I see SHE goes in there all the time, and I can see her asleep in the round window. I want to try that, too.

And just maybe there could be some of her special food. I must follow her some night to see where she goes.

I don't see food outside, like at my old place, but she must be fed.

The human called Charlie is coming out and going over to another small house further down the lane.

Actually, I see my old house from here. I feel kind of sad – I like the kids who live there.

Sometimes one of them would sneak me upstairs into her bed. I really liked that, but that wasn't often. Most of the time, I slept outside in the barn with all of the other creatures. I would rather have the nice warmth of inside the house.

Maybe if I follow Charlie, he will let me into his house.
He still keeps on telling me to go home, that he doesn't even like cats, but I can feel from his hand on my neck that he really likes me – he just doesn't know it (yet).

Wow, I just got a glimpse of Alice out of the corner of my eye.
So she lives here with Charlie.
She sees me, too. This is not good. But I bet she gets her food here.

Okay, now things are looking up.

Perhaps if I hang around the door, Charlie will let me in, or I can sneak through his legs...

My life with the human called Charlie

Mornings in the big house by the warm fire,
Charlie is chatting with the other humans,
and I am getting lots of pats.

Life is very sweet.

SHE is being a bit nasty, but she leaves me alone.

Did I tell you I even have my own dish, which she eats from sometimes, but I also eat from hers.

We even sleep in the red barn near each other, but she is not liking my move in.

She hisses at me whenever I am near her. Oh well.

I still haven't caught a fish, but there are lots of bugs and birds that hang out at the pond, and the humans sometimes go in the water and float.

I don't like to get wet, so I have to be careful not to fall in while trying to get me one of those dragonflies.

All good things come to those cats who are patient, and that's me.
I believe I have arrived at my forever home.

My favourite thing of all to do with Charlie is ride with him on his electric scooter. We go up and around all the trails in the woods. I jump off and explore, and he just sits and chats to me. He holds me tight on his lap when we hit rough spots – I really like that.

Life is good, and did I tell you? I just love my forever home up over the hill with Charlie!

MAX SAYS: A few facts about cats

- House cats share 95.6% of their genetic makeup with tigers.
- Cats jump 5 times their own height.
- Most cats have 18 toes: 5 on front paws, 4 on back paws .
- The whiskers on a cat are like a kitty radar, especially at night.
- Cats sleep about 15 hrs a day.

Manufactured by Amazon.ca
Bolton, ON

34722738R00024